An American River Almanac

REFLECTIONS
ON NATURE
THROUGHOUT
THE YEAR

Acknowledgments

The author gratefully acknowledges the many people who generously shared
their expertise when these essays were originally written or reviewed their accuracy
when the material was updated for this book. All remarkably knowledgeable in ways
of the river, they include Jack Hiehle, Jim Jones, Jack Wilburn, Ed Littrell,
Bill Grenfell, Fred Gunsky, Bruce Swinehart and Ed Harper.

Kim Mueller provided legal guidance to the American River Natural History
Association for this book.

The essays of Peter J. Hayes are reprinted with the permission of
Ralph Danel Jr., last publisher of *The Sacramento Union.*
All photographs are reprinted with the permission of the photographers.

ISBN 1-887815-11-2

Proceeds from this book will benefit the mission and goals of the
American River Natural History Association.

Designed by Gail Segerstrom
Printed in Hong Kong

An American River Almanac

REFLECTIONS ON NATURE
THROUGHOUT THE YEAR

Peter J. Hayes

TEXT BY PETER J. HAYES

PHOTOGRAPHS BY TOM MYERS & GEORGE TURNER

The American River Natural History Association
Carmichael, California

In memory of Carol Lou Hayes
and dedicated to all who follow the river

The nonprofit American River Natural History Association supports nature interpretation along the American River Parkway and financially assists the programs of the Effie Yeaw Nature Center in Sacramento County's Ancil Hoffman Park. ARNHA maintains a gift shop at the Nature Center with proceeds dedicated to its mission. Membership applications are available at the Nature Center and www.arnha.org.

Other publications of the American River Natural History Association:

A History of the Lower American River
Birds of the American River Parkway
Ooti, A Child of the Nisenan
The Outdoor World of the Sacramento Region: A Local Field Guide
Stories Effie Told
Biking and Hiking the American River Parkway
Discovering the American River Parkway (A Field-trip Guide)

Contents

Preface

SACRAMENTO arose at the confluence of two rivers.

The muddy Sacramento is the workhorse, stretched south from the delta in concrete traces to nourish crops and populace. It is life-sustaining. But the sparkling American is life-affirming. Its melted snows slosh from the Sierra through the forks of white-water canyons that once lured gold miners and now sport rafters. It eases into the respite of Folsom Reservoir, then Lake Natoma, then tumbles past the salmon and steelhead hatchery that substitutes for its once-natural spawning beds.

As it becomes the Lower American, it ripples along a 30-mile urban greenbelt of American River Parkway before finally joining the Sacramento. There a jagged band marks where the clear waters of the American resist turning darker.

It is in celebration of the American River and the plant, animal and human life it fosters that this book is offered.

An American River Almanac was created from time-stained newspaper clippings that Peter Hayes saved from his days at *The Sacramento Union* newspaper. As an editor in the 1970s and 1980s, Pete would pen reflections on local fauna and flora to break up the editorial pages' daily diet of opinion.

He tucked away published copies of these nature editorials and eventually had hundreds. Pete retired in 1990 and *The Union* expired in 1994. The clippings grew brittle.

Two years ago, Pete handed over his stacks of yellowed essays to the American River Natural History Association for republishing, perhaps in an illustrated book, with proceeds to be dedicated to ARNHA's mission to promote interpretive education in the American River Parkway.

The final product, this *American River Almanac*, is blessed with the striking photography of Tom Myers, George Turner and Jack Wilburn. It breathes

fresh life into more than 60 of Pete's editorial musings on the river region. Minor edits included updating the species' names. Placement of the pictures flows like the river.

ARNHA's Board of Directors extends its appreciation to Pete and to Ralph Danel Jr., the last publisher of *The Union,* for permission to reprint the editorials.

The Board also expresses its deep gratitude to the widely respected nature photographers whose remarkable generosity enabled this book to evolve from concept to reality. Their artistic photographs and Pete's fine essays are so well matched that at times it seems their works were designed for one another.

For that we also are indebted to Gail Segerstrom, who selected the art from thousands of nature slides that Tom Myers and George Turner made available from their separate collections. Jack Wilburn added his slides to fill our gaps.

When all was done, nature editorials that once stood alone were paired with pictures and put together chronologically, beginning with New Year's Day. The result tells a verbal and visual story of the seasonal rhythms of the river. It builds from the cold silence of winter through the pleasures of spring to a crescendo of activity as the river dances in summer's heat. The tone inevitably turns golden on the way to another foggy winter. Ever-repeating, ever-changing, these ceaseless cycles offer their own subtle lessons.

Here are the kingfishers, golden eagles, coots, salmon, beaver, bullfrogs, deer and other creatures of the river's environs. Here is the still life—the cottonwoods, poison oak, wildflowers—that give texture to the river's edge. Even the roiling skies are captured in words and photographs.

As these pages testify, each darkened year portends a rebirth. It's not unlike the way faded words on crumbling newsprint spring to life with each new reading.

—Rebecca LaVally, *Publications Chair*
American River Natural History Association

Winter

Nature's rhythm

IT IS A MINT-FRESH New Year for those inhabitants of the globe who use the 12-month calendar devised in the 1580s by Pope Gregory XIII. But for the flora and fauna it is just another day in the timeless rhythm of the seasons. It was winter yesterday and it will be winter tomorrow.

As nature's timekeepers—the sun, the moon and the stars—draw us closer to spring and summer, the western fence lizard hardly stirs as it hibernates under a rock in the Sacramento Valley. It will know enough to waken when the temperature starts to rise.

The mule deer that spent the summer in the high country is enjoying the hospitality of the Sacramento region until the snows recede. There are no New Year's fresh starts for this long-eared mammal.

But our most visible wild animals, the birds, show the continuous quality of the seasons. Canary-like goldfinches flocked to the dried star thistle yesterday and you can be sure they'll be back tomorrow to glean its seeds. Kingfishers with bushy "punk rock" crests will continue to play tag along the river, calling raucously. Coveys of quail will hunker down in wild blackberry patches, ready to burst forth and startle unwary hikers.

And so it goes. Grasses that were bright green in December are just as verdant in January. Buds continue to swell in willows and cottonwoods along the rivers, and even a few wildflowers are brightening the winter landscape with blossoms, such as the lanky telegraph plant's clusters of bright yellow daisies.

No, there was no need for blaring horns or clocks striking midnight to signal a fresh start for nature's world. The animals and plants kept to their own seasonal schedule dictated by the sun, moon and stars. The five-year-old chinook salmon found its way back to its American River birthplace, spawned and died. In an oft-troubled world, we are thus assured that in nature there is a quality of life that is at once seamless and predictable.

The western fence lizard will know enough to waken when the temperature finally rises.

Animal engineers

WE DON'T OFTEN SEE the largest of rodents in daylight, but we know it's been around. A white alder lies flat next to the river, and around its chiseled stump lie piles of wood chips. In the nearby shallows is a dome-shaped structure made of twigs and mud. It's the comfortable lodge of the beaver, the workaholic of the animal kingdom.

It's said to be the only animal that changes its environment, thanks to large front teeth that keep growing even as they wear down. The beaver uses its teeth to cut trees and branches for its lodge, to throw up a dam to impound water, to strip the inner bark of trees for its food.

And when there are no longer trees near the water's edge, this animal engineer digs canals in which to float food and building materials to river or lake.

The breed is a descendant of animals that played a key role in the opening of the West. Their lush brown fur was the magnet that attracted hardy mountain men such as Jedediah Smith to the American River and other hunting grounds in the 1820s in quest of the rich pelts destined to become fashionable hats for men.

February is the mating season for beavers, most of which are believed to stay together for life. Most litters are born in April or May, averaging four kits to the litter. They will be raised in the upper chamber of their lodge, accessible via an underwater entrance out of reach of predators. As the young near their second year, their parents nudge them out of the lodge in a not-so-gentle hint to go start their own new colonies of eager beavers.

*With its ever-growing
front teeth, the beaver
never misplaces its tools.*

Winter forms

ALONG THE RIVER the cottonwood trees described by John Charles Fremont fork near the base into several trunks and lean toward the water. Their heart-shaped leaves have long since fallen, exposing a thick whitish bark on stout branches, and a tracery of twigs against a cold gray sky. Also exposed are sickly green clumps of mistletoe.

We glory in the firs, pines and other evergreens that brighten the winter landscape. But as any easterner will tell you, there is something to be said for the transitory nature of deciduous trees and their bare-boned silhouettes.

When Fremont first noticed the cottonwood that was to bear the U.S. Army explorer's name, on January 6, 1844, near Pyramid Lake in present-day Nevada, it proclaimed the presence of welcome springs in an arid land. He wrote that he, Kit Carson and others in his party regarded them as harbingers of a better country, and today we view them as harbingers of spring.

There also are smaller but more shrubby willows lining the watercourses. With their leafless gray stems, often red toward the ends, they suggest a line of smoky flame between land and water.

Serving as accent to the naked willows are symmetrical, white-barked alders adorned with dangling catkins, those pencil-like clusters of yellow flowers that precede spring's leafing out. Then there are the native sycamores, with thick, gnarled branches, some virtually sprawling on the ground. Frosty bark flakes off the limbs of this "brotherhood of venerable trees" that soon will display leaves like those of a maple and big as a man's hand.

But no discussion of native deciduous trees in winter is complete without calling up the vision of the valley oak, highest form of vegetation in our area. It may reach 100 feet in height, and its wide-angled limbs stretch 100 feet across. It is the monarch dominating the valley landscape, as much in winter as in summer.

There is something to be said for the transitory nature of deciduous trees and their bare-boned silhouettes.

Droll one

THE RUDDY DUCKS, the goldeneyes and the Canada geese are among the thousands of waterfowl loafing through the winter on valley ponds, rivers and lakes. Paddling among them is a slate-gray little bird we'd be tempted to call an odd duck, except it isn't a duck but a funny old coot.

People can't help laughing at the American coot, its head and white bill bobbing backward and forward as it chugs across a pond. Its croaking call has been compared to an ungreased wooden axle. And when it takes flight, its enormous feet skitter across the water and its stubby wings flap frantically before it staggers into the air, recalling the line from World War I air combat movies: "You're not going to send a kid up in a crate like that, are you?"

*American coots'
rubber-ducky routines
are worth a laugh and
a half.*

The coot is a member of the rail family that is usually found in marshy areas. It's also called a mud hen and, if one wants to get fancy, an ivory-billed mudpecker.

With spring, most of the ducks, geese and swans will have headed back to the north country to raise their families. Not the coots. Most of them will hang around the valley, build nests of shallow baskets among the reeds and produce baby coots that are even funnier-looking than the parents. A bald crown surrounded by a muff of orange-tipped feathers, an even brighter shawl over the neck and shoulders, a reddish bill and those snowshoe feet add up to what seems a Walt Disney creation.

The gregarious coot may not have the grace of a swan, the rainbow hues of a wood duck, or the flying skill of a pintail. Nor is it popular with farmers. But give it high marks for its ability to adapt and its entertainment value.

Mystery voices

A ROLLING, MUSICAL "c-r-o-n-n-k" signals the presence of one of the more distinguished wildlife visitors to the delta these winter days. Like all cranes, the sandhill crane has a long windpipe that amplifies its voice a mile or more. From a thousand feet, from behind a levee, the sound of a bird that is heard but not seen is carried on the blustery January wind.

Then they come into view, a half-dozen ash-gray birds flying flat out, their long necks not kinked like a heron's. One of the six, obviously a young hot-pilot type, goes into a partial wingover just as they reach out with long black legs for a field of rice stubble. There they keep up their rippling call, inviting other cranes in the neighborhood to come on over, pickings are good.

The 4-foot-tall sandhill crane may not have the p.r. of its endangered cousin, the snowy-white whooping crane. But it does have its fine points, such as a red cap above a white face and a bulge of long feathers drooping from its lower back like a ballerina's tutu.

Indeed, the crane is something of a dancer itself. During the upcoming mating season, the big birds will flap their wings and hop, skip and jump as much as 10 feet in the air in their courtship ritual.

The cranes have been here since October, using long, sharp bills to feed on roots, bulbs and large insects in the grasslands. About mid-March, they'll start out for their breeding grounds in eastern Oregon and northeastern California. If you hear what sounds like the musical croak of a long-winded frog, look up. It may be sandhill cranes on their way home.

During courtship, sandhill cranes like to dance up a storm.

It's the berries

NOW WE BECOME conscious of the stirrings of spring, thanks to full days of sunshine following on the heels of soaking rains. Lushly green grass covers soggy river banks, a reminder that lawn-mowing time is approaching. And from a tangle of bare brown branches, tender shoots of leaves sprout forth. The blue elderberry is one of the first of deciduous plants to awaken from a winter's sleep.

Little leafy green candelabras no bigger than a baby's thumb rise from the long branches of this member of the honeysuckle family. As the weeks go by, these sprigs will unfold into compound leaves with finely-toothed leaflets, food factories for an all-purpose native plant.

Blue elderberry shrubs
offer a bountiful table
for riverside wildlife.

In April, the elderberry will send forth clusters of flat-topped, creamy white flowers. Then come the blue-black berries, usually covered with a waxy coating and relished by songbirds and band-tailed pigeons, along with rabbits, mice and chipmunks. Deer browse on the leaves.

Native Americans called the elderberry the tree of music because they made flutes from sections of the branches. They used hot sticks to push out the soft pith, leaving a thin woody shell. The ancient Greeks also knew how to make a musical instrument from the elderberry. They called it a sambuke, from which the shrub derived its Latin name, *sambucus.*

It should be pointed out that except for the blossoms and berries, the elderberry is poisonous. And even the berries must be cooked. Then, rich in Vitamin A and protein, they make quite acceptable pies, jellies and jams. Countless folks will testify to the merits of elderberry wine, for medicinal purposes, of course.

Success story

IT HOVERS 70 feet over the valley grassland, a graceful white bird with pointed wings that beat steadily. By its color and contour it resembles a gull—but a gull doesn't hover like that, does it?

Its kite-like silhouette and its long white tail are clues to its identity. It is a white-tailed kite, whose classic whiteness belies the fact it is a bird of prey. This handsome member of the hawk family is making an encouraging comeback after having dwindled to an estimated 50 pairs early in the last century.

Kites threatened to follow the dodo into extinction as the result of the old-time human hobby of collecting their eggs (whitish, spotted red and blackish brown) and the bad reputation, often unwarranted, that all hawks were "chicken hawks." The kite's distinctive color and hovering, trusting behavior made it an easy target for marksmen.

Full protection under state law and greatly increased irrigation and cultivation of farmland reversed the kite's trend of diminishing numbers. The birds have returned the favor and are now considered good friends of farmers, especially grain-growers.

Hovering over a field, the kite spots a meadow mouse moving along a runway between entrances to its underground burrow. The hawk sideslips to the ground feet first, seizes the mouse in its talons, and soars upward. Since a meadow mouse eats the equivalent of its weight in vegetation each day, and if left alone would multiply at a prodigious pace, the white-tailed kite makes a key contribution to the balance of nature.

After a day of hunting, the kite returns at dusk to a communal roost in a tree, where 40 or more will spend the night. Later in the spring they will pair up and build nests high in the trees. They do not migrate.

Fortunate is Sacramento to be one of the centers of California's kite population, an all-too-rare success story of a wildlife species that graduated from the rare and endangered list.

The white-tailed kite has made a comeback after threatening to follow the fate of the dodo.

*The steelhead is
a well-traveled
trout.*

Super Trout

THESE ARE DAYS when the sight of fishermen standing hip-deep in the swirling waters of the lower American River reminds us anew of the miracle of the anadromous fishes. These are the fishes that are born in fresh water, swim downstream to the ocean and return to the same stream to spawn. They include salmon, sturgeon, striped bass, shad, and the currently most-sought-after species, the spendid steelhead.

(We always had trouble with the word "anadromous" until we finally looked it up. It's pronounced *a nad' ra mas* and is Greek for "running upward." Its opposite is "catadromous," which describes fish such as eels that migrate downstream to the sea to spawn.)

The fisherman who comes home with a 10-pound or so steelhead can be excused for feeling like a latter-day provider in the tradition of Daniel Boone. The "steelie" is the seagoing version of the rainbow trout, widely regarded as "the fightingest trout," a subspecies of which is known to have taken the rugged ride through the turbines at Shasta Dam and migrated to the sea and back.

Anglers will swear there's nothing to compare with the

experience of having a steelhead take a baited hook and bolt away on long runs and spirited leaps out of the water. If lucky, the fisherman will eventually conquer his prize on the banks of the American, possibly near the gravel nest where the steelhead entered the world as one of some 4,000 eggs several years ago.

During its lifetime a mature steelhead may survive threats ranging from loss of oxygen caused by silt when it was only an egg, to disease, to countless predators such as bigger steelheads, great blue herons, seals, and sharks.

In the ocean, it grows sleek on plankton, crab larvae, squid and other fishes for two or more years. Then a reproductive spark signals that it is time to return to fresh water. Navigating by the sun or the stars, the steelhead finds its way to the mouth of the Sacramento and then the mouth of the American, and from there an incredibly acute sense of smell guides it back to its place of birth, either in a gravel bed or the state Fish and Game hatchery at Nimbus Dam. Unlike its kin, the salmon, which dies after spawning, the steelhead usually lives to migrate to sea again, unless it ends its life in a fisherman's net. Either way, the steelhead is a very well-traveled trout.

Storm's aftermath

WITH A LIQUID MOTION, a muskrat slips from the water onto a half-submerged branch by the river's edge. Cinnamon-brown fur almost hides its beady eyes as it peers about in search of a succulent root during an uncharacteristic daylight feeding foray. Then it drops back into the water and heads for home under streamside tree roots.

The plump rodent's easy movement matches the placid flow of the Lower American. The river is behaving itself on this overcast February day, a far cry from last month when it surged over its banks as warm rains melted the Sierra snowpack.

How far did the river surge over its banks? The evidence is there, 10 to 15 feet up the slope, where the untamed water carved small canyons in trails, uprooted trees and broke off branches, spattered blackberry leaves with mud and left a bathtub-like ring halfway up the trunks of stout cottonwoods.

The storm may have left the landscape in disarray, but we see evidence of a resilient life force. Two coots glide across a pond left by the receding river, while a staccato squeak signals the presence of a woodpecker exploring a massive oak, and bent on gleaning insects.

The deep soaking followed by sunshine hastened new growth from the battered ground. Elderberry canes are now garbed with bright green sprouts shaped like fleurs-de-lis. Poison hemlock, beautiful with its finely divided fern-like leaves, pokes up through the dead brown floor. Also appearing is the mugwort with its soft-green leaves, so pungent when crushed.

Thus does nature demonstrate its fickleness, hitting with a k.o. punch with one hand and picking us up with the other. There's nothing boring about the seasons in the big valley.

Behind the riparian scene of trees, new life forces mark the changing season.

Call it capricious

SO FAR FEBRUARY is living up to its reputation for eccentricity. Clashing weather systems have spawned thunder, lightning, reservoir-filling rains, even a tornado in our valley. By the almanac, it's the last full month of winter, and let's not forget it!

February is sort of a johnny-come-lately month. The first Roman calendar devised by Romulus contained 10 months, and February wasn't among them. But Romulus's immediate successor, Numa Pomplius, legendary second king of Rome, added two months, making February the last month of the year. The name comes from *Februarius*, a Latin word meaning to purify. It seems the ancient Romans purified themselves in February to clear the decks for New Year's revelry.

Julius Caesar shifted the beginning of the year from March to January, but purification is still a good symbol for February. The wind-whipped rains sweep across the valley floor, setting the stage for March's vernal equinox and spring. Surely the good rains mean we'll have a bumper crop of poppies, lupine and other spring wildflowers.

Meanwhile, purplish-pink giraffe's head blossoms are showing up on grassy meadows. Out on the river handsome mergansers paddle sedately. Occasionally they head for the bottom, seeking small fish to grab with their long thin bills. Before May these diving ducks will depart to raise families at wooded lakes in the far north and in the mountains. There, no doubt, there will be a change in the weather—to frigid. To each his own.

Handsome mergansers paddle sedately, but may head for the river bottom.

Wood Ducks

IT'S NOT EASY catching a glimpse of the valley's most beautiful duck. Wintering goldeneyes, wigeons and buffleheads dive and dabble out from the shore of stream or lake where it's easy to pick them out.

But the gaudy wood ducks are more bashful. They cling to the shoreline, sheltered among tules and overhanging willow and cottonwood branches. They're pairing up now, which accounts for the sudden splashes as one drake drives off another that has tried to "cut in," so to speak.

The male looks as if he's on his way to a clown convention. A long, slicked-back crest crowns a head that's a riot of color— green, purple, chestnut, white and black. He has red eyes and a partly red bill.

The female's plumage is more subdued. But when it comes to spring house-hunting, she's in charge, darting through the treetops along the water's edge, searching for a tree hole suitable for a nest. Sometimes the one she settles on is the same cavity in which she laid her eggs last year.

She adds to the cottonwood's interior decor with down plucked from her breast. One day, not long after the 10 or so eggs are laid and hatched, she will fly out of the hole and call to the young. One by one, they will claw their way up the side of the cavity and tumble out, like a string of paratroopers hitting the silk. Down they'll flutter, landing on the ground or water, rarely to any harm. For these flamboyant fledglings, it's almost duck soup.

The resplendent wood duck is often hidden by streamside plants.

Shy ones

THE TIME IS APPROACHING when mule deer bucks will be traveling about bare-headed, having gone through the mid-winter ritual of shucking off their forked antlers. By early spring they will start growing a new set that will once again overshadow the mule-like ears for which they are named.

But chances are, only the fisherman or other early risers will be aware of this metamorphosis. The shy animals usually venture forth from their American River Parkway refuges to feed only during the early morning and late evening hours.

Unfortunately, only a tiny remnant of mule deer is left in the river bottomlands where multitudes of deer and antelope once played. Heavy hunting almost exterminated the pronghorn antelopes in the 19th century, with a few thousand surviving today, mostly in Modoc and Lassen counties.

For grace, beauty and gentility, the mule deer is hard to match.

But while civilization has chased most of the deer from the Sacramento region, they have found new homes in the Sierra foothills, and by summer they will have migrated to the high country. Careful management by the state Department of Fish and Game, financed by hunters' license fees, has very likely resulted in greater numbers of deer today than existed in primitive times.

But back to the antlers. When a new set starts growing, it is covered with a velvet-like skin until fully developed into a fine hat-rack. Then the skin is shed, and by the time mating season begins in the fall, the antlers will be shrunken and hard.

Gawky, spotted fawns will arrive on the Sierra scene by mid-July, when tender new greenery provides nutritious feed. Does carry their young for about seven months, and among older does, twins are more common than single births.

For grace, beauty and gentility, the mule deer is hard to match. Wildlife experts estimate that there may be as many as 600,000 deer in California, and while we may not see them often, it's nice knowing that they're here.

Song in the air

LIKE MANY of its winged brethren, the oak titmouse is raising its voice in spring song these days. And a good thing, too, since without its lively, melodic whistle floating from the live oak branches we might not be aware of this well-camouflaged bird as it moves with acrobatic ease through the trees, gleaning insects and seeds. It's gray above and whitish below, with a pointed crest its only distinguishing mark.

To hear it sing, anyone might suspect a whole flock of birds inhabits the tree. Many variations on a theme bubble forth, not the least of which is the *chick-a-dee-dee* that is easily confused with the notes of a chickadee. And it rarely stops singing.

All of which points up the fact that no other member of the animal kingdom lets itself be heard as much as birds do. Some of them spend half or more of their waking hours singing, and

The titmouse may be advertising for a mate when it sings sweetly.

the principles of natural selection suggest they wouldn't be using up all that energy unless it helped them survive.

So what makes the little titmouse sing? According to biologist Joel Carl Welty, it may have something to do with a bird's reproduction. Maybe it's advertising for a mate and demonstrating its vigor. Or it may be establishing sovereignty over a nesting territory. Or, and this is our idea, maybe the proud father is celebrating the arrival of six to eight titmice. Only the males sing.

Other reasons may have to do with a bird's social functions. Its vibrant song may be a password for species identification. Or it may be trying to drive away enemies or competitors.

There also could be more individualistic reasons. The titmouse may be simply engaging in voice practice, just like any opera star. Or maybe it is singing from a sense of well-being, simply for the joy of it. Anyone who likes to sing in the shower can understand that.

March is ...

MARCH IS THE MONTH of the vernal equinox, when the sun is directly over the equator marking the end of winter and the advent of spring. Officially it occurs around March 21 but we all know it really happens when chilly breezes yield to a friendly sun, followed by that abundant capital city species, the lunchtime lawn-lounger.

March also is fruit trees bursting forth with heavily-scented blossoms. It is the rose-colored flowering quince, the pollen-flecked catkins of the willows. And the honeybee loading up with pollen and nectar, all the better to help members of the plant kingdom reproduce, and to make honey to share with other members of the animal kingdom.

March is the hidden meadowlark's song rising from the drab expanse of last year's star thistle. It is three kestrels playing the courtship game above the cottonwoods, until one male gives another the message that three's a crowd. It is gulls floating high overhead in lazy white circles against an azure sky.

March is long grass sprouting from the river bank, showy stands of mustard and not so showy specimens of wild radish.

It is wild ducks and geese heading back up the Pacific flyway to Arctic tundra nesting grounds. It is bears and chipmunks emerging from a long winter's nap. It is, alas, mosquitoes.

March also is the mourning cloak, one of the first butterflies to come out of hibernation and compete with the honeybees for nectar from the willow flowers. (There's enough for all.) Its wings are a velvety dark brown, edged in yellow, hardly as dispiriting as its name implies. More fitting is the name it is given in Britain: the camberwell beauty.

March is so many good things, but mostly it is the stirrings of spring with the irresistible urge to sing out: Welcome back!

The mourning cloak is one of the first butterflies to emerge on the river landscape.

John Muir saluted incense cedars for sheltering stormbound birds and hikers.

Spicy evergreen

CINNAMON-BROWN, deeply furrowed, fibrous bark covers a trunk that is widely buttressed at the base and tapers to 150 feet above the forest floor. Its scaly leaves are arranged in fan-shaped sprays on gracefully curved branches.

It is the incense cedar, and it would be understandable if a newcomer to California confused it with a young Sierra redwood, mightiest of trees. The incense cedar is a splendid species, but not in the same class with the redwood—just as in the race for glory, few of us remember the names of the astronauts who followed Neil Armstrong to the surface of the moon.

However, the incense cedar shouldn't be sold short. It is far more widespread than the Sierra sequoia, thanks to winged seeds that are highly tolerant of shade or sun. September winds carry seeds released by slim, cylindrical cones far from the parent trees, and seedlings spring up in profusion.

Now the seedlings are covered by several feet of snow, but with the spring runoff a water-soaked ground will speed their growth, along with spurring the pines and other conifers.

The incense cedar well deserves at least part of its name. Not "cedar," because it's not a true cedar but rather a member of the cypress family. But wherever it grows, even in home gardens, it brings the aroma of incense, thanks to leaves and seeds that contain pungently odorous resin.

Incense cedars may grow to be 1,000 years old, making them mere youngsters compared with the living-fossil Sierra redwoods that have seen 3,000 winters. But that lyrical naturalist John Muir could be counted on to find a fitting superlative for the incense cedar, as when he described its distinctive "plumes" of foliage.

He wrote:

No waving fern-frond in shady dell is more unreservedly beautiful in form and texture or half so inspiring in color and spicy fragrance. In its prime, the whole tree is thatched with them, so that they shed off rain and snow like a roof, making fine mansions for stormbound birds and mountaineers.

Here's spring!

IT'S SPRING AGAIN, and the male hummingbird goes into its pendulum display, giving the old come-on to a passing female. High into the air he climbs, pauses and plummets toward the ground on 200 wing beats a second. (A pelican lumbers along at little more than one wing beat a second.)

Just as he appears about to crash into the ground, the metallic green hummer levels off with an explosive *chenk!* from his outspread tail feathers. Then, up, up and away like one of the Air Force's vaunted Thunderbirds. Could anyone ask for a more spectacular entrance for spring?

Perhaps so, if one is a wildflower fancier. Then the nod might go to shooting stars, lavender-to-maroon and sometimes white members of the primrose family now making an appearance along the north fork of the American River and in other moist spots. Oddly, the petals fold backward, revealing the maroon

The hummingbird:
Could anyone ask
for a more
spectacular
announcement of
spring?

and yellow throat and stamens that are often joined together, accounting for another name, mosquito bills.

Add more seasonal indicators: clouds of goldfinches, bright yellow plumage flashing, descending on fuzzy white seedheads of star thistle. A white-crowned sparrow feasting on the catkins of a willow tree. And buttercups, Indian paintbrush and manzanita with its pink, urn-like blossoms emerging in the understory along the path.

There's nothing new about all this activity along the riverbank. But it's always encouraging to see how the imperfections of a modern society fade before signs of the pulsing renewal of life itself.

Spring

Buddy system

THE VERNAL EQUINOX made its annual return last week, to no one's surprise. Spring is officially here, so we celebrate the beginning of plant and animal growth, tangible evidence of life's renewal.

It won't be long before we can admire nature's foresight in arranging the birth of the badger, the gray fox and the mule deer at the same time nutritious shoots of greenery emerge from the ground. This happy symbiosis makes itself felt in other ways. Helping encourage the growth of plant life are animals such as nectar-seeking honeybees and hummingbirds that also pollinate the flowers.

Squirrels, by stashing acorns underground, assure that new oak trees come to life. And the beaver that dams a mountain stream floods the surrounding terrain and permits moisture-loving trees like willows and alders to get started.

Of course, food is the prime benefit that plants provide animals, as when milkweed plants play host to the caterpillar that eventually is transformed into the far-ranging monarch butterfly.

Occasionally animals repay in kind, providing food for plants, as when the cobra-like pitcher plant traps insects inside its hollow leaves. The result: more nitrogen for the plant.

When a quail scratches for grubs beneath a wild blackberry bramble, it is taking advantage of another benefit that plant life offers animals—a protective covering from the elements and predators.

But more than any other members of the animal kingdom, the farmer, the gardener and the florist maintain a buddy system with plants. We benefit from plants' nutrition and beauty while storing the seeds and bulbs, planting, watering, fertilizing and harvesting them.

Nor should we humans forget that many animals have served our kind from the beginning. Perhaps the best way to return the favor of symbiosis is to avoid driving plant and animal species from this Earth.

Buddies:
honeybee and
dandelion.

Healthful horehound

THE SPRING SUN is warming the river-lands soil, damp from the returning rains, and plants are starting to pop. The seeds, the bulbs, the perennial roots that have been set out by the careful gardener are responding to the seasonal impulses in their proper location.

Also the weeds.

Somebody said a weed is any plant that grows where you don't want it. Grass is great when it is a neatly mowed lawn, but it qualifies as a weed when it sprouts in a rose bed. And oats in an oat field are a valuable crop, but when they sneak into a cornfield, they're pesky weeds.

Ralph Waldo Emerson had a more optimistic view: *What is a weed? A plant whose virtues have not yet been discovered.*

But this version doesn't apply to common horehound, even though most people simply would say this member of the mint family is a straggly plant with woolly green leaves that grows wild along the rivers and in the foothills. Immigrants brought horehound from Europe along with recipes for its use as a home remedy in the form of candy and tea.

Its flavor? There's a clue in the Latin name, *Marrubium vulgare,* with *Marrubium* coming from the Hebrew meaning "bitter." Edible-plant guru Euell Gibbons referred to its "musky bitter" flavor. Someone who tried the candy was reminded of cough drops, but that's as it should be since it's good for sore throats and coughs.

So let's not call horehound a weed. It's a medicinal herb!

European immigrants prescribed horehound as a home remedy.

It's that time

A SPARROW HOPS about under a tree on a downtown street, fills its beak with dried grass and flits to the branch of the honey locust tree. After a moment or two of surveying its surroundings, it darts in a line across the wide thoroughfare, its destination the ledge of a stately bank building. It's as good a place as any to raise a family.

These are busy times for birds as they enter the breeding season by building an infinite variety of nests. The idea is to safeguard themselves, their eggs, and their young from predators and bad weather during the most vulnerable time of their life cycle. Even so, fewer than half of the chicks born this year will reach maturity.

Inaccessibility is the goal of phoebes and swallows that nest on girders beneath bridges, the kingfisher that digs a hole deep into the side of a cliff and an African bird known as the water thick-knee that simply lays its eggs next to a crocodile that also is brooding its eggs on the sandy shore of a river. Now that's inaccessible!

Most nest-builders are camouflage artists. Kinglets use mosses and hummingbirds use lichens to cover the outside of their nests. Some species, such as the killdeer, bring off the ultimate in camouflage chutzpah by building no nest at all; they simply lay protectively colored eggs on the bare ground, and if a predator approaches, go into a raucous broken-wing act to lure the intruder away.

Nor does an emperor penguin need to build a nest to keep its solitary egg off the Antarctic ice. It rests the egg on top of its webbed feet, covers it with a warm fold of belly skin, and incubates it while waddling about.

Some avian architects such as orioles build nests with roofs to protect the young from rain, sun and sandstorm, in addition to predators. The more tightly constructed the nest, the warmer it is, thus enhancing incubation in concert with the heat supplied by the brooding parent. As a result, the young develop more rapidly, reducing their vulnerability and increasing their life span.

Baby mockingbirds and their brethren are always hungry.

Flying colors

IT'S A TOSS-UP these days whether a certain member of the woodpecker family is seen or heard first.

The northern flicker is a jay-sized bird that wears a coat of many colors. Perched on a cottonwood snag, it shows off a brown back, a black crescent across the chest, numerous black spots on white underparts, and the male sports red sideburns. When it flies, it flashes salmon-red colors under the wings and tail, along with its trademark, a white rump.

While the flicker is no song stylist, it signals its presence with a yelping call that carries the sound of its name long distances through woodlands and suburbia. And about now it may be heard drumming on a tree trunk, drilling a nesting hole with its chisel-like bill.

For a flicker, raising a family can be more stressful than for most birds. After moving into a freshly built cavity to lay her eggs, the female may be joined by a pesky starling with the

The northern flicker is an avian fashion plate.

same thought in mind. The flicker is usually evicted by the aggressive starling in one of nature's less desirable practices, which has reduced the population of flickers, at least hereabouts.

But ordinarily the flicker doesn't spend as much time in trees digging out insect larvae as do other woodpeckers. Indeed, it's the only woodpecker that forages on the ground, hopping awkwardly about and using its long sticky tongue to search out its favorite food, ants.

Over the years the flicker has had colorful local names. In the West, it's sometimes called the red-shafted flicker for its wing and tail feathers, which were used for native vests and headdresses in ceremonies. The eastern variety was known as the yellow-shafted flicker.

It is also called high-hole, red hammer, yocker bird, wilcrissen and wake-up. The last name refers to its occasional practice of drumming on rain spouts and wood siding of houses in the pre-dawn hours. At such times even the flicker's most ardent admirers might decide that this avian fashion plate would be better seen than heard.

New beginnings

APRIL CAN BE a world-class month, especially after what seems like 40 days and 40 nights of cold, miserable wetness.

April is white clouds stacked up like billowy snowdrifts above the Sierra, it's a green mist of new growth on willows, it's the querulous cries of magpies squabbling in the cottonwoods.

April is a warm pullover made of sunshine. It's daffodils struggling upright after being knocked askew by recent rains.

It's leafing through seed catalogues and garden books, wishing the ground would hurry up and dry out.

April is the delicate but deadly lacework of new-growth poison hemlock leaves. April is a pair of mallards upended in a pond like toy ducks. April is the perpetual motion of a saffron-colored butterfly.

April is the grassy ground carpeted with filaree, tiny pink flowers of the geranium family that may be a part of our history. From an indispensable field guide, *The Outdoor World of the Sacramento Region*, we learn that the Maidus are said to have offered filaree greens to Captain John Fremont and Kit Carson to eat after they had made a hard winter crossing of the Sierra.

April is the gray-green Lower American carrying kayakers smartly downstream.

April is the sibilant symphony of tree swallows performing acrobatics around their cottonwoods homes. April is the season of renewal and of new beginnings.

April is clouds stacked up like billowy snowdrifts.

Ladybug, ladybug

ASK A QUESTION like, "What's good for keeping aphids off roses?" and you get a variety of replies. There are plenty of insecticides, but have a care. Go the organic way and plant garlic next to the roses. Or enlist a praying mantis. Or ladybird beetles, also known as ladybugs. Aphids, look out!

Let's salute the ladybug, everybody's favorite beetle, half the size of a pea, orange wings speckled with black dots, a flame-colored fragment amid the garden greenery.

Chances are that some of the local ladybugs have just arrived from the Sierra Nevada where they spent the winter hibernating in swarms of thousands under a log. The next step is to lay eggs on leaves near a mass of aphids. The larvae hatch and start feeding on the aphids, which to ladybugs are akin to apple pie a la mode. After polishing off several thousand aphids, the larvae will soon be tranformed into the familiar, brightly colored adults.

*Colorful ladybird
beetle or ladybug
is the special
friend of gardeners
and farmers.*

Unlike the cucumber beetle and other black-hatted beetles that destroy growing crops of fruits and vegetables, most ladybug varieties are beneficial to man. How beneficial, California citrus growers found out early in the century.

Something called the cottony cushion scale insect was accidentally introduced into California from either Australia or New Zealand. It killed hundreds of thousands of trees, threatening the entire orange industry of the state.

The government sent entomologists to Australia and they brought back 140 little Australian ladybugs that were turned loose on a few trees. Within 18 months, they and their progeny had controlled the scale infestation.

Our state insect is the dog-faced butterfly, and no doubt it deserves the accolade. But if anyone wants to pick a state beetle, here's a vote for our good friend, the ladybug.

Wild oats

PALE GREEN SPIKELETS of wild oats droop in loose clusters. Lengthy brownish hairs hanging from the ends of the spikelets make them look like long-legged insects with folded wings. Although it has been a dry winter and spring, this annual grass has headed out early, ready to fill niches in our valley's life-support system.

Cluck-cluckers have borrowed the name of this European immigrant to help them describe a young person who lives too fully if not too wisely. It's easy to see why. Having arrived mixed with crop seed or tangled in the wool or hair of introduced livestock, wild oats are among the most opportunistic of plants.

As livestock that was introduced during California's early rancho period cropped its way through the palatable perennial natives, wild oats and other weedy annuals moved in and took over. Today few native grasses remain. The passing of the native grasslands and the introduction of agriculture has meant, in turn, the passing of once-abundant tule elk and pronghorn antelope.

But wild oats and other introduced annual grasses have proven to be highly nutritious forage for livestock and smaller animals. Rodents such as the San Joaquin kangaroo rat and goldfinches and sparrows eat the seeds. Gophers drag stems, roots and foliage down into their burrows. Nor are jackrabbits choosy about what parts of the oat plants they eat. Grasshoppers and other insects eat their share, too.

There need be no fear that all this pressure will spell the end of the wild oat. It reseeds itself prolifically, and the herbivores that feed on it are kept in check by hawks, coyotes and snakes.

Need more proof of the wild oat's value? Well, it binds the soil together, preventing erosion. And there's the aesthetic factor presented by green and golden seas of grass "as soft as the breast of doves and shivering-sweet to the touch."

Wild oats, non-native annuals, pay their way as nutritious forage for livestock.

Color it blue

WILDFLOWER FANCIERS ARE A HARDY LOT, hiking miles across field and meadow, scrambling up hillsides, armed with hand magnifiers, all the better to identify a *Platystemon californicus* (cream cup), or some such.

But the non-purist can enjoy spring's messengers equally well just by looking about. No wildflower puts on a more dazzling show than lupine as it covers patches of our valley floor and roadsides with a blanket of blue.

From California's mountains to its deserts to its seashore, this colorful member of the pea family comes in more than 80 varieties. There are many others elsewhere in the country, including the Texas state flower, the bluebonnet ("with the dew on it").

The five-petaled blue flowers edged with white are shaped like bonnets, marching one above the other along the stem. And the leaves are what botanists call palmate form, shaped like a hand and its fingers reaching out to the sun.

One should not be put off by the fact the name comes from the Latin for *lupus* or wolf. For some reason, the Romans thought it robbed the soil. But the opposite is true. In fact, lupine restores nitrogen to the soil, and with its long roots it was planted to stabilize the sand dunes on which San Francisco's Golden Gate Park was built. Honeybees are great fanciers of the nutritious pea.

So look for the lupine as you walk the river region. If lucky, you may see them mixed with golden poppies, surely one of our premier spring spectacles.

Lupine's five-petaled blue flowers edged with white are shaped like bonnets.

May Time

ALL OF A SUDDEN it's May, and where have we been? It's just that the seasonal rush of new growth brings an overwhelming awareness of the month's intentions. In Thomas Hood's words, *O'er the earth there comes a bloom; sunny light for sullen gloom.*

It's a blooming month all right, and not just for wildflowers. Take the buckeye tree or shrub, all covered with creamy plumes of flowers looking like white lights garlanding a Christmas tree.

Flat-topped clusters of pale yellow flowers cover blue elderberry shrubs up to 10 feet tall. The blossoms presage the arrival of dark blue berries that the Maidus prized as relish for dried salmon or deer meat and pioneer women used in pies and jellies.

A blizzard of white blossoms crown tangled blackberry bushes in moist woodlands near the river. While the elderberries aren't too tasty raw (and their red cousins aren't edible at all), there's no question of the flavor quotient of blackberries that will soon be along. We're told that blackberrying was a pleasantly productive diversion for valley youth in the early days.

Then there are sweet-smelling clovers, the ever-spreading vetch, a pea family member whose unimaginative name fails to do justice to its purplish-red flowers; and clumps of purple-headed milk thistle whose seeds promise tasty fare for goldfinches this summer. Not to be overlooked, cottony masses of ripened flower seeds drift to the ground from female cottonwood trees.

Finally, the wild roses are blooming up a storm, light pink blossoms offering a delicate counterpoint to stout, thorny branches. No *May*be about it—it's a bedazzling season bespeaking a generous earth.

Clovers add a sweet-smelling dimension to the river region's landscape.

Vernal pools

WILDFLOWERS LIGHT UP the landscape, speaking a language of spring in the big valley. And nowhere is that language more articulate than around the vernal pools in our urban area backyard.

Southern Oregon and South Africa are the only other areas where climate, topography and soil characteristics come together to set the stage for these flower-ringed pools. But the pools themselves have become endangered species.

A vernal (spring) pool gets its start from the layers of hardpan formed in the Central Valley soil that is more than half a million years old. Winter rains from our Mediterranean-type climate accumulate in the depressions that dimple the terrain.

As the rains diminish and water evaporates, a typical pool is transformed into an ever-changing oasis of color. The shoreline slowly shrinks, signaling successive species of wildflowers to flourish under the changing conditions. Here, on the quick-

drying edges, are the yellows of goldfields and yellow carpet, followed inwardly by the whites of meadowfoam and popcorn flower, until finally on the bottom of the pool near the center are blue displays of downingia. All are destined for a four-month life cycle.

Before settlers came, vernal pools and even vernal lakes were found in profusion on the valley floor, along with grizzly bears and tule elk. Levee-building, farming and other developments have replaced them.

The Fair Oaks Recreation and Park District is credited with preserving perhaps the best example of vernal pools in Sacramento County. They lie in Phoenix Park on Sunset Avenue, east of Hazel Avenue, and professional and amateur botanists use them and others as outdoor laboratories.

A vernal (spring) pool is formed when rain collects over layers of hardpan in certain soils.

Sierra spring

VIOLET-BLUE LUPINE and golden poppies blend in the red dirt banks on the side of the road. A red, yellow and black western tanager flashes through the oaks. A tawny young deer steps carefully across a road, then bounds off into the brush.

If one hasn't rediscovered the natural world and cool freshness of a spring morning in the Sierra foothills, this could be the day to do so.

One place to find it is along Auburn-Foresthill Road as it cleaves the peninsula between the north and middle forks of the American River above Folsom Lake. It is picked up at the Auburn Ravine Road exit from Interstate 80 a couple of miles above Auburn.

The road curves gently upward through rolling ranch country, offering spectacular views of the American River Canyon. The traveler with a sense of history might imagine riding a swaying stagecoach with 1850s Argonauts en route to the Jenny Lind gold mine in Foresthill.

Side roads, such as the Old Foresthill Road beckon. On foot along wooded trails, one discovers countless wildflowers such as the buttercups with their lacquered-yellow petals and Latin name *Ranunculus* which, we are told, means "little frog," signifying that buttercups, like frogs, like water.

Beyond Foresthill, take the road to Michigan Bluff where Leland Stanford had his store before becoming a railroad builder, governor and university founder. Study the sooty-gray dipper as it flies low up and down a tumbling stream, even pausing to walk under water. Round a curve and see "the enchanted dogwood with its ivory trays."

No, the city-bound valley resident ought not delay in welcoming a Sierra spring's promise before it melts into summer.

Golden poppies complement spectacular views of the American River Canyon.

Tough Bird

IN A THICKET of cottonwoods, a menacing form perches on a branch. Deep shadows conceal its coloring, but the cat-like silhouette is a giveaway. Two feathery tufts project upward and outward from its massive head, heralding the presence of the great horned owl.

This is one of the biggest and baddest of predators, but in the late morning hours it is somnolent. In Northern California, the great horned owl is often found in the same areas as the red-tailed hawk. But the big birds don't get in each other's way, since the hawk hunts in the daytime and the owl takes the night shift.

Now, as someone approaches it, the owl spreads wings that have rust-brown undersides and span four or five feet. An intruder watching it wheel silently through the trees would appreciate the fact it was retreating in the opposite direction.

Consider the tools that the great horned owl brings to the task of checking the rodent population in the course of finding its food. For one, its large, yellow eyes point forward, unlike those of other birds, permitting it to focus on an object with both eyes. It depends even more on its remarkable hearing equipment to find its prey in the dark. The owl's wide head comes in handy, too, enabling the owl to detect the direction of a sound by determining the differences in intensity with which the sound strikes each ear.

And a great horned owl can swoop soundlessly down on unwary prey, thanks to its billowy flight feathers that are muffled by comb-like projections and fringes. Finally, it is equipped with sharp talons and beak.

Perhaps because of their wide-eyed appearance, owls have been regarded as symbols of wisdom since the days of ancient Greece. Alas, experts tell us that geese, crows and ravens have more smarts than the "wise old owl." Still, when the great horned owl sits on a branch uttering its measured four- or five-hoot call, it's a rare and foolhardy creature that ventures into its territory.

A great horned owl can swoop soundlessly down on unwary prey.

Spring colors

THE TANGLE of bare-boned elderberry branches appears lifeless against the blue sky. But suddenly a tiny object at the tip of a branch flashes orange, then crimson iridescence as the sun ignites the colors on the head and throat of a hummingbird.

Such are the colorful revelations that shimmer in the parkway woodland in the heart of the metropolitan area. The colors are a sparkling counterpoint to the lush green thickets of willows, cottonwoods, elderberry and poison hemlock, the latter a towering member of the parsley family that would dwarf a professional basketball player.

Closer to the ground, a yellow-and-black swallowtail butterfly staggers purposefully through the air to a clump of filaree. There is no sign of a nectar shortage among these dense-growing plants.

Now a hawk with a rusty-red tail soars toward a cottonwood branch and its collection of twigs that can only be a nest. There is a gap in the feathers on the bird's right wing, possibly the result of a thoughtless marksman, but the feather gap fails to hamper the big raptor. It is carrying a lifeless mouse as it lands in its nest and is greeted excitedly by two fuzzy white chicks with dark eyes. It is lunchtime for the baby red-tailed hawks.

Colors abound from nature's palette—an olive-green bullfrog that is more than a foot-and-a-half long, a trio of yellow-breasted western kingbirds playing aerial tag in a three's-a-crowd routine, a red-headed house finch collecting seeds from a thistle, and gray-brown California quail herding a covey of young along the trail.

Some of the colors are for camouflage; others are to attract a mate. Whatever their purpose, they are the vibrant grace notes that enliven the springtime wildlands.

A red-tailed hawk adds a rusty dab of color to a perfect sky.

Doting mom

COMPARED TO her resplendent mate, she is something of a shrinking violet. Her plumage is a dusky mottled brown. He boasts a glossy green head and neck, white collar, chestnut-purplish breast and gray flanks. Everyone recognizes this river rogue in his breeding plumage—the male mallard.

But the female of the species has a few redeeming features. For one thing, she can out-quack her reedy-voiced mate. This talent is useful when it is necessary to sound an alarm to her young if hawks, large fish or other danger threatens.

Now is the time to see the doting mother mallard with her brood on the lower American River. Suddenly they appear from the shore upstream, heading purposefully on a diagonal course across the smooth-flowing waters, a dozen fuzzy yellow-brown ducklings in a line followed by the mother. They reach the shallows on the other side, dabbling head down to feed on grasses and other vegetation.

She doesn't let them get too far away because the balance of nature is ever-changing here on the river. The odds favor only half of the ducklings growing to maturity.

And where is the father? Earlier he threw himself into the wing-flapping, head-bobbing courtship ritual, and stayed with the hen until the nesting period began. Then, like other male ducks, he went away.

But later in the summer he molts into the same drab plumage as his abandoned mate. That transition is called the "eclipse," which may keep him from getting too uppity.

The mallard hen's plumage is drab—and her mate's will be, too, before long.

River Walk

THE MATURING SPRING seems to signal a stepped-up tempo of natural rhythms along the river. What better example than five male mallards, glossy-green heads and necks tipped upward, wings beating furiously, flying in close formation under a bridge like a flight of jet-jockeys?

A yellow swallowtail butterfly with black wing margins and black tiger stripes hurries through shrubby willows along the shore. Pale pink blossoms presage the juicy sweetness of wild blackberries, a reminder of what the Maidus and pioneers knew, that the best of life is free.

The booming *jug-o'-rum* of a bullfrog echoes from a hidden pond, apparently indicating its availability for parenthood. Without even seeing him, we'd risk 40 dollars that he can outjump any frog in Calaveras County. And a tiny wren flits through the underbrush, wagging its tail from side to side, singing high, singing low, trilling counterpoint to the bullfrog's resounding call.

The bright green, feathery leaves of sweet fennel tickle yet another sense. Squeeze one and it gives off a fine licorice fragrance; come back in a month or two and savor the tasty seeds, which folks in the old country long ago discovered enhance cookies, soups and stews.

Overhead, bits of cottony masses from the tall cottonwoods drift like lazily moving gulls against the bright blue sky. Fleets of snowy cumulus clouds are anchored near the horizon, slowing down all the action of a late spring day.

Big, streamside Fremont cottonwoods shelter nesting birds, raccoons and squirrels.

Proud oaks

ON OUR VALLEY and foothill landscape, the valley oak is the climax plant, the highest form of vegetation in the region. It reaches up to 100 feet tall, its graceful limbs spreading in broadly symmetrical sprays.

The valley oak's cousins, the interior live oak and blue oak, also flourish in the valley and Mother Lode.

"Sweet and agreeably flavored," was Lt. John Fremont's report on tasting acorns in a Maidu village on the American River in 1844 as his expedition neared the end of the first winter crossing of the Sierra.

Acorns were a staple in the diet of the natives who lived in the valley and foothills. Today in oak groves along the American River, one can find flat boulders or rock outcroppings pock-marked with holes made many years ago by Indians rotating stone mullers to grind acorns into flour. Acorn meal was made into bread, or a soup or mush called atole, used even today in Maidu ceremonials.

As people spread over the valley floor, the splendid oaks dwindled in number. More than a dozen fine specimens can be seen at Sutter's Fort. And many Sacramentans have discovered that the oak makes an excellent garden ornamental, since few insects bother it and it grows faster than one might think.

Who cares if oaks are too brittle for commercial uses, as long as they provide shade, beauty and a rich heritage?

Native oaks offer beauty and a rich heritage.

Summer

Partners

AN EVER-MOVING black fragment swoops and darts, silhouetted against the blue sky over Folsom Lake. Suddenly it alights on the glowing orange head of a western wallflower to sip nectar and you see its wings are not black at all, but an iridescent blue-green.

It's the pipevine swallowtail butterfly, a prime example of how an insect's life cycle can mysteriously interlock with that of a plant. For this beautiful swallowtail has established a partnership with another interesting Northern California native, the Dutchman's pipe. This vine spreads 5 to 10 feet along the ground and up and around a tree or shrub. And it boasts a spectacular blossom, curved to resemble a Dutchman's pipe.

Spring has been a little late this year and many wildflowers are two weeks behind their customary blooming period. But not the Dutchman's pipe, whose blossoms started appearing in March. For some unknown reason, the pipevine swallowtail will select this plant on which to lay its eggs from May through July. Then comes the marvelous metamorphosis to larva, or caterpillar, then pupa and finally adult butterfly. The tender

leaves, stems and seed pods of the vine provide breakfast, lunch and dinner for the hungry black caterpillars with orange spots.

Our valley's warm summer months hurry the pipevine swallowtail through two or three life cycles. It's a short life but a merry one for this fluttering jewel, and we should hope that nothing threatens the Dutchman's pipe, the butterfly's perfect host.

Host to the pipevine swallowtail butterfly, the Dutchman's pipe leaves no doubt about the origins of its name.

Spring again

IN THE BIG VALLEY, the Lower American is alive with rafters, the hills are parched yellow, and the almanac says the days are growing shorter. But one of the advantages of living by a mighty mountain range is that one can turn back the calendar until it's spring again, a reborn maiden with flowers in her hair.

Under the lodgepole pines 6,000 feet above the valley floor, the lacquered petals of buttercups and lush grass present a panoply of gold and green. The buttercups are right at home in the moist ground, among the first plants to flower as the Sierra snows recede.

Equally acclimated are small yellow violets nestled under shrubs close by a rushing creek. A butterfly, its black-dotted, orange-red wings fluttering madly, hurries across the landscape. (The two species represent a fine symbiotic relationship—the violet's leaves afforded an important source of food for the butterfly in its earlier caterpillar stage.)

Nor is this the only such winged jewel. There is a large black-and-white swallowtail and a black, white and orange Lorquin's admiral butterfly. Not to mention a "floral butterfly," the Mariposa tulip. *Mariposa* is Spanish for butterfly; this profusely growing member of the lily family with its lavender-tinged white petals barely rises above the ground.

And there are wild buckwheats with sulfur-colored heads, forget-me-nots that mirror the blue sky, pink pussy paws and royal purple larkspur, all in a single patch not much larger than a flatlander's backyard. If one should venture farther north, or south, or higher, or lower, or come back to the same spot a month from now, there would be many more wildflower varieties, all celebrating the Sierra Nevada's spring festival.

If one should come back to the same spot a month from now, there will be even more wildflower varieties.

Echoes of Thoreau country

THE POND IS HIDDEN by a curtain of willows and cottonwoods a couple of dozen frog-jumps from the river. Its murky brown surface is shrinking under the impact of the July sun, exposing a muddy shore where green whiskers are sprouting. The air is still.

If, as Thoreau said, the perception of beauty is a moral test, the pond offers infinite challenges to the eye. Dragonflies skim over the surface like low-flying crop-dusters, searching the air for small insects. These hungry predators are well-equipped, having four gauze-like wings and beady eyes that cover most of the head, letting them spot a mosquito at 15 feet.

Unseen bullfrogs taking the sun return to their watery homes with a loud *plop*. White butterflies seek out nectar-carrying plants. An intruder's sense of solitude is broken by the reedy hum of a male cicada as it "sings" its invitation to females. He is vibrating plate-like membranes at the base of his abdomen, but it does no good to try to locate him in the foliage of the willows, as he is a master ventriloquist.

A tiny warbler vanishes into a thicket, a killdeer probing the mud for aquatic animals takes flight with a startled cry, a kestrel hovers on beating wings high overhead. In the distance the intermittent drumbeat of a woodpecker provides a rhythmic accent to the natural symphony in this suburban Walden.

With large, spherical eyes, dragonflies can zero in on a mosquito at 15 feet.

River's edge

THE RIVER SLIDES quietly through the suburbs, a slender shadow of its usual self. But there's enough sun-splashed water to float a rubber raft full of happy teenagers, and plant and animal life crowd the shore, providing business-as-usual in the natural world of the riparian woodland.

A host of dragonflies, their legs arranged to form a handy basket, pluck insects from the air. Spiny yellow star thistles are everywhere, seemingly with few redeeming features until it's noted that they are visited by nectar-seeking bees. The blue flowers of a member of the mint family play a similar role for an orange-and-black painted lady butterfly.

A placid pool comes alive as egg-sized tadpoles are disturbed and thrash their way into deeper water. Nearby are peers that have developed the long hind legs, along with a fully formed, bulging-eyed bullfrog.

A husky brown flicker lands in a blue elderberry shrub, performing gymnastics on a slender branch as it picks off clusters of blue-black berries. Burbling finches likewise enjoy the shrub's berry smorgasbord.

Wildflowers thrive under the benign influence of moist soil and the July sun. Here are snapdragon-like yellow monkey flowers, tiny but fragrant sweet clover, and the remarkable evening primrose, with 6-foot or higher stems with bright yellow blooms that open at dusk but shrivel under the next day's sun.

There's no slowing the pulsing cycle of life at home on the floodplain.

A bullfrog eyes
his watery scene.

State Bird

A FRIEND REPORTS seeing a pair of California quail shepherding six offspring across a side street off busy Eastern Avenue. The family made it safely across the street, but there's no telling how they fared thereafter. Since a normal brood numbers 13 to 17, those six were apparently the lucky survivors.

Whether these quail grow up will depend on whether their striped and downy coloring escapes the eyes of predators, as nature intends. If no shelter is available, baby quail do have a last resort—the knack of "freezing" so they may blend into natural surroundings like spotted fawns in the woods.

This species, California's state bird, is a personal favorite because it sometimes raises its family out where people can see it, in suburbs and parks. As summer progresses, several families may join forces in a covey that moves like a company of camouflaged troops through the underbrush as its members forage for seeds and insects.

The adults, gray-brown with white trim, also know something about protective coloration. And there's no mistaking the California quail with its bobbing topknot, shaped like a large black comma. Or is it an apostrophe?

The parents gather their scattered flock with a rapid clicking call that sounds like a series of "giddy-up" signals to a horse. In a few months the young will be able to fly up into trees to avoid some of their predators. But with their short, round wings and long legs, they spend more time on the ground like their cousins, barnyard chickens. Their call is a loud *chi ca' go.*

At one time, California quail were one of the most common birds in the state, but unlimited bags by market hunters drastically reduced the population. They've been making a comeback since before the beginning of the last century, thanks to clearly defined hunting seasons and bag limits. So there's something to be thankful for—that our state bird hasn't gone the route of the passenger pigeon.

The quails's topknot: a comma or an apostrophe?

Throwback

THE POND TURTLE is an olive-brown lump on a rock, stolidly taking the sun, a reptilian exponent of Satchel Paige's dictum that to live a long life it is necessary to avoid the social ramble and other unnecessary exercise.

This must work, because the turtle lives a long time—as long as 25 years. It's an armor-plated throwback to the Mesozoic era 200 million years ago when dinosaurs stomped the earth.

But now the valley's only native turtle bestirs itself. The salad-plate-sized animal drops into the water in quest of a meal of insects, small fish or water plants.

If it happens to be a female, this is the time for her to crawl some distance away and use her claws and feet to dig a small hole in a stream bank or hillside. There she will lay five to 11 hard-shelled eggs and cover them with silt. Two months later, the young will hatch and make for the water. Beginning in November, all of the turtles will hibernate beneath the mud under the water until February.

All of which provides an excuse for recalling Ogden Nash's ode to the bony-shelled reptile: *The turtle lives twixt plated decks, which practically conceal its sex. I think it's clever of the turtle in such a fix to be so fertile.*

The female pond turtle claws a nest in a stream bank and lays five to 11 eggs.

River running

Canoeists match forces with the river.

THERE ARE TWO basic ways to sense the dimensions of the lower American River as it winds through the capital city and environs. One is to pick a spot on the bank amid the willows and cottonwoods and watch the product of Sierra snowfields slide by en route to the Sacramento River and, eventually, the Pacific.

That is the role of the spectator and to sit is a pleasant experience indeed. But more involved is the participant who, with the help of an inflated rubber raft, canoe, kayak or inner tube can become a part of the final run of the river from which the gold rush sprang.

For the participant, the Lower American is a river of many moods on its 23-mile sweep to Discovery Park. Released from Folsom Dam, Lake Natoma and then Nimbus Dam, the American moves past green galleries on either shore, picking up speed as it splits to race by on either side of a gravel bar.

Slowing the tempo, the river spreads out and meanders past a rocky shore of gold dredge tailings where a lone killdeer steps carefully and utters the shrill call that gave it its name.

Sometimes the river flattens out so the unwary traveler misses the main channel and scrapes bottom for a few moments before pushing off into deep water.

Past high cliffs dotted with holes made by home-building swallows, the river-runner is paced by a belted kingfisher sounding its rattling cry as it dives for fish. Overhead, an acorn woodpecker with flashes of white-and-dark wings shuttles back and forth across the river, from treetop to treetop.

Now there's a new sound—an insistently steady roar. Up ahead the river seems bumpier than usual, then there is a flash of white water signaling the San Juan rapids. Soon the life-jacketed traveler is into the rapids, into water slipping glassy smooth over slanting granite slabs, pitching downward and outward, a moment of no control, swirled toward the shore.

Just as suddenly the downriver journey resumes placidly, and the river floater is joined by multi-colored dragonflies and tiger swallowtail butterflies, moving past shore greenery, propelled by a relentless force, one with the river.

Blackberries

IT IS A BOUNTIFUL YEAR for wild blackberries hereabouts. A member of the rose family, the blackberry by any other name would taste as sweet.

It covers dense thickets along rural roadsides and in moist areas, and if there is a more valuable wild fruit than the blackberry we don't know it. Nor did the Maidus and pioneers who gathered them along the American River. Among early-day Sacramentans, blackberrying was the thing to do at community picnics.

So what if the leaves and stems are thorny? Such obstacles are easily surmounted in gathering a fruit so rich in Vitamin C. The blackberry's delicious blend of tartness and sweetness is savored while being picked, later with cream and sugar, or as one of the great desserts of all time, blackberry pie with vanilla ice cream. And let's not forget blackberry jams, jellies, cordials and wines.

Birds and mammals also pay homage to the wild blackberry. Its brambly growth provides protective cover and the berries, of course, are food for towhees, squirrels and other wild creatures.

Luther Burbank, the Santa Rosa plant wizard, developed a white blackberry so transparent that its small seeds could be seen. Wonder why he went to all the trouble to try to improve on perfection?

California blackberries belong to the rose family.

The river

THE AMERICAN RIVER has meant much to many. First were the Southern Maidu or Nisenan, whose villages were located throughout the 2,000-square-mile American River basin. Their men speared or dip-netted salmon that were eaten fresh or smoked and dried for the winter. Their women used the fibers of nearby redbud trees to make unsurpassed baskets with diagonal or zigzag designs. Their medicine men tried to rid pain with the aid of guardian spirits said to inhabit the river.

In 1808, Spanish explorer Lt. Gabriel Moraga and a party of soldiers and padres became the first white men to see the river. Moraga saw the snowcapped Sierra in the distance and watched the river waters churn through a rocky gorge, which

Modern-day explorers navigate the rapids of the north fork of the American River.

reminded him of the sufferings of Jesus during the crucifixion. He named the river Las Llagas (the wounds).

The years passed and Jedediah Smith and his mountain-men beaver trappers camped alongside the river; then John Sutter erected his famous fort on a rise overlooking it. Mexican Governor Juan Bauista Alvarado named the river the American in 1837, with reference to the Yankee trappers who frequented it. John Fremont and westering settlers followed the American out of the mountains. And James Marshall found gold nuggets in its sands on a cold January morning in 1848, thereby transforming the American into one of the most important rivers in the world.

Today the gold is mostly gone, but the snow-fed waters of the American continue to bestow riches on Californians. There is water to nourish the fields, electricity to light the homes, and brawling rapids, placid sweeps and fishing holes to refresh minds and bodies. Always there is its song: Keep it clear, keep it clean, keep it flowing.

Season's gold

AS THE DAYS dwindle down toward September the landscape takes on a golden aura bespeaking the riches yielded up long ago. Golden grasslands, golden wildflowers and an occasional golden cottonwood leaf mark the season in the Nature Area of Sacramento County's Ancil Hoffman Park. Many of the signs have their reason for being, too.

See the head-high, woolly spike standing like a sentinel in the wild grasses. A rosette of leaves encircles the common mullein's stalk and a mass of buds, seed pods and yellow flowers crowd its long head. Ancient Greeks and Romans dipped the stalks in tallow and used them for funeral torches. Today hummingbirds collect hairs from the leaves for nests and goldfinches feast on the seeds in late fall.

Then there are the rounded heads of yellow flowers on the feathery sweet fennel. The four-foot-tall plant looks like asparagus, smells like licorice and is used as a flavoring in cooking.

High overhead looms a green shrub of thin, needle-like branches topped by clusters of yellow, fragrant flowers. It is Spanish broom and was used by early settlers who bound the branches together to make household brooms.

Close to the ground is the dandelion, with bright yellow flowers on hollow stalks and jagged-toothed leaves that supposedly look like a lion's teeth. In our lawns it is a much-maligned weed, but here it holds wildflower status. And of course its greens are good to eat in salads.

And floating on the park's tree-ringed pond is a network of yellow water weeds, a bright flower belonging to the evening primrose family. It's important, too—its stems play host to eggs of the dragonfly, which eats mosquitoes and other insect pests.

Taken together, we admire the fading summer's golden-headed cast of actors that play key roles in the balance of nature and brighten the land.

The landscape of late summer grows golden.

The Lorquin's admiral won't be around much longer this year.

Metamorphosis

EARLIER IN THE YEAR it was a drab, mottled-brown caterpillar. It looked like it had two heads in front of a pair of horns and a row of bumps, a bizarre appearance possibly designed by nature to confuse birds, lizards and other predators.

But like most butterflies, the showy Lorquin's admiral has come a long way since those creepy-crawly days. With its brown-black wings, pure white band and orange wing tips, it looks like a refugee from a Halloween party. And it won't be around much longer this year.

It belongs to the largest family of butterflies, *nymphalidae*, along with mourning cloak, buckeye, painted lady and the admiral's look-alike, the California sister. Its name honors a Frenchman named Pierre Lorquin, who came to California as a gold-seeker in the 19th century, had no luck, and made his reputation if not a fortune as a butterfly collector. "Admiral" is part of the name of other butterflies too, possibly because their bright colors evoke an admiral's uniform.

Each year, three generations of Lorquin's admirals inhabit moist meadows and long streams from the valley floor up to the Sierra's lodgepole-fir belt. An egg laid this fall will hatch into a caterpillar that feeds on the leaves of willows or cottonwoods. It hibernates through winter, rolled up in a leaf like a cigar.

Lorquin's admiral diverts its enemies in numerous ways. It creates dummy caterpillars by using its silk to hang up the skins it has shed, fooling predators. In its third stage, as a hard-shelled pupa, its many colors mimick bird droppings.

When the brilliant butterfly finally emerges from the chrysalis, it flies with rapid wing beats, alternately gliding, as it searches for nectar from blossoms of button bush, goldenrod, aster, thistles and coyote bush. At the same time, it helps pollinate the plants.

Intensely territorial, it usually returns to the same perch. The male chases off other Lorquin's admiral males and other species and tries to mate with the Lorquin's admiral females that enter its area.

Unlike the famous monarch, Lorquin's admiral doesn't migrate, just lives and dies as an adult in only two weeks. It's a short life but a colorful one for this winged flower.

Heard but unseen

SMALL JOKE: For the person with a suppressed desire to walk the primrose path, now is the time to do so with no risk at all. No, not the bard's primrose path of dalliance, but the American River Parkway path flanked by evening primroses. The butter-yellow, poppy-like petals open up at sundown and by the middle of the next day they have withered. Meanwhile, long buds are swelling preparatory to bursting into bloom at nightfall.

It is a nice exercise in sustained yield by nature, and it has been going on most of the summer, illuminating a path that by no means leads to irresponsible decadence. It is a riverside course shared with occasional young cyclists, puffing joggers and a perceptive stroller who points out the looming silhouette of a great horned owl perched on a cottonwood branch.

Most of all, it is a place to let the mind slip into neutral, forgetting about the price of gasoline and other day-to-day irritants. If there is any concentration at all, it is to wonder why you can hear a small creature rustle in dry cottonwood leaves but never see it, why the noisy magpies here have yellow bills, while magpies everywhere else have black bills, why a lizard sheds its tail and why we've had such a splendidly salubrious summer. Why indeed?

The mournful call of the killdeer draws our attention to the river, but there again nature has hidden its presence.

The river is alive with fishermen standing on either side of the channel, chest-deep, trying for steelhead. They are silent, and although we watch for many minutes, we never see them catch one of the prized seagoing rainbow trout.

Fishermen too are enjoying a special primrose path, a sort of back-to-basics sojourn on a mildly warm September afternoon.

With its loud, mournful call, a killdeer is often an unseen presence along the river.

War paint

THE APPROACH of autumn may cause transplanted easterners to start missing the brilliant colors of the season back home. But not to worry. The valley and foothills do offer swatches of red and orange foliage, although we're talking here about poison oak. You take your fall color where you find it in this Mediterranean-type climate. Unfortunately, poison oak's brilliant colors do not lend themselves to table decorations since their leaves give off oil particles that irritate the skin of those who are allergic.

This feature is embodied in the old-fashioned warning, "Leaflets three, let it be; berries white, hide from sight." Each poison oak leaf stem contains three lobed leaflets that resemble the leaves of our native oaks, although poison oak is not an oak but a member of the sumac or cashew family, and a cousin of the East's poison ivy.

Poison oak's whitish or brown berries often remain on the shrub all winter, providing important food supplies to woodpeckers, magpies and other birds. They aren't affected by the plant's poisonous qualities, just as rabbits, deer and bears can browse on the leaves with impunity.

Poison oak's fall war paint reminds us that most early-day American natives also were immune to the plant. The juice from its leaves and stems turns black on exposure to the air, and the natives used it as a dye in designs worked into their beautiful basket-making. But for most of us, poison oak must remain a look-but-don't-touch accessory to the fall landscape.

Poison oak warning: "Leaflets three, let it be."

*The garden spider likely
built its web
in darkness.*

Garden engineer

DRAPED BETWEEN two branches of a willow is a slender silk web, illuminated by the sun, orb-shaped, a masterpiece of symmetrical beauty. Right in the center clings the black-and-yellow spider that created the web, waiting for an unwary fly or mosquito to happen by.

This is a prime time of the year to admire the handiwork of the web-spinning engineers in gardens, parks and along the rivers. They're among the few animals that make traps to snare their food. And though the traps appear gossamer-thin, they have enormous elasticity and a tensile strength greater than steel. It's said that a rope of spider's silk one inch thick could suspend 74 tons.

Very likely the garden spider built its web under cover of darkness. The silk is produced by glands in the abdomen. The animal uses its hind legs to draw the silk from "spinnerets" located near the abdomen on the undersurface. As soon as the silk comes forth it hardens quickly. The spider attaches a sticky strand to one branch, then fastens the other end to another branch. It then crosses back and forth over the bridge, putting on additional strength to hold up the web. A box-shaped frame

is created, then a series of spokes leading to the center, followed by sticky spiral strands from spoke to spoke.

The female usually spins the web and catches the food. The female also produces silk to serve as a large sac in which to protect her eggs from the weather.

Thanks partly to poor public relations, such as the widely publicized incident involving Miss Muffett, the spider is a much-maligned member of the animal kindom. It will bite if anyone is so imprudent as to manhandle one, but only the black widow and the brown recluse are poisonous. On balance, all are highly beneficial to humans, helping to hold down populations of pest insects such as the gypsy moth and cotton worm.

Who could ignore the tale of Scottish hero Robert Bruce, who learned to overcome failure by watching a spider try again and again to fasten a thread? Finally it succeeded and the inspired Bruce went forth to victory in battle. So it's said.

Expert angler

SOME OF THE green herons that came into the world this summer have started for Mexico. But a few will spend the winter in their American River Parkway haunts, and catch the eye of alert hikers and cyclists.

It's odds-on that John Sutter and his crew of Kanaka oarsmen spotted the green heron as their boats wandered through the delta's tule marshes in 1839 in search of the Sacramento River. It's the smallest of the family of long-billed, long-necked, long-legged wading birds.

About the size of a crow, it stands on a cottonwood snag protruding over the water, its neck hunched, eyeing an intruder. A close look at it discloses a shaggy greenish crest, chestnut neck and bluish back. In breeding season its bright orange legs are a giveaway, but they're greenish-yellow now.

Most of the time the green heron stands stock-still as if asleep. Then a frog or marine animal gets careless and the bird's spear-like bill darts forward to grab it.

It is one of the few birds to use a "tool" to catch its food. Like a fly fisherman, it drops a feather into the stream and, when a fish rises to grab it, pounces.

When startled, the heron takes off with a series of protesting *kuck-kucks,* its legs trailing, its wings flapping vigorously. Elsewhere in the country, down-home birdwatchers call it "fly-up-the-creek."

Green herons may not be as showy as other members of their family, such as the snowy egret or the stately great blue heron. But in the midst of a busy urban area, these slim, solitary birds are right at home by the water's edge.

The green heron drops a feather in the water to lure a hungry fish, then spears it.

It's coming

THE OCTOBER WIND rustles the cottonwood branches, releasing a yellow leaf that flutters to the ground. It lodges in a tall telegraph plant, a gold coin of autumnal beauty.

A chunky brown bird flies silently over the thistles, its white outer tail feathers identifying it as a meadowlark. If this were spring, it would be making rhapsodic song, proclaiming the season of awakening for all manner of animals and plants.

Not that there are no birds singing now. There is the yelp of a flicker, the lisp of a titmouse and the croak of a coot as it prepares to dive beneath the surface of the river. Not to mention the squawk of a jay, whose flashy blue, gray and white plumage helps to balance its anti-social behavior.

As the colors begin to turn, fewer birds are making themselves heard.

Most wildflowers have become dried stalks, except for the telegraph plant's clusters of daisy-like blossoms, blue vervain with its tiny lavender-blue flowers, and sweet clover, which perfumes the air.

Recently a brush fire swept through this wild land by the river, blackening the ground and scorching shrubs and trees. Despite the fall season, the fresh greenery of Mexican tea, mugwort and coyote bush is reclaiming the devastated ground. Dragonflies hover like mini-copters over the curving skeleton of parched blackberry branches. A monarch butterfly offers a brilliant orange accent to the rejuvenated area.

Actually, fall has been a little late this year. That accounts for the late crop of mosquitoes, which in turn explains why dragonflies are present in large numbers. Anywhere else it would be a case of Mother Nature slowing down, getting ready for the big sleep. But not here.

Autumn

Autumn by the river

ON AN AUTUMN river walk, not everything is as it seems. The apparent blade of dried grass opens its wings and becomes a lemon-yellow butterfly. Large, many-colored "eyes" on the brown wings of another butterfly deter hungry predators. Similarly, black marks behind the ears of a perching kestrel resemble eyes to large hawks flying over this smallest of falcons.

Even the tall shrub with spikes of tiny lavender-blue flowers isn't what it seems to be. It has square stems, just like members of the mint family. But actually, it's blue vervain, from the family of *verbena*, Latin for the holy bough carried by priests.

However, most of the verities of autumn are just as they seem. Coppery dragonflies hover over willow leaves. Butter-yellow blossoms of evening primrose begin to unfold, resuming an unusual 24-hour cycle that ended at mid-day as neighboring blooms withered. And a green heron stretches its chestnut-colored neck as it takes flight across a grass-ringed pond, squawking with annoyance at being disturbed.

The late-afternoon sun weaves a skein of diamond lights that dance on the river's surface. The current swirls around an angler standing waist-deep in the river, hoping for a trophy steelhead. And a flock of gulls holds a conference on a nearby gravel bar, one of them raising a plaintive *kee-yah, kee-yah* point of order.

And the cottonwoods. How better to expose the senses to the changing season than to scuff through a pile of their dried, parchment-like leaves, evoking a blend of sight, sound and sensation that might have inspired Norman Rockwell to paint a woodsy pathway leading into Americana.

The decaying leaves are in the midst of a process that will return their nutrients to the soil during the coming rains, feeding the roots of the tall, water-loving trees. No false colors for the cottonwoods, which are just what they seem to be.

Buckeye butterfly's multi-colored "eyes" help it ward off predators.

Busy bird

THE YELLOW-RUMPED warbler, perpetual-motion sprite of the visiting winter birds, is back in town.

Smaller than a sparrow, the yellow-rump was formerly known as the Audubon's warbler. The current name should be a tip-off to its most distinctive feature, bestowed at the price of a salute to the 19th-century Boswell to birds, John James Audubon. (The western sub-species retains Audubon's name, however.)

At this time of year, its coloring is a dull brownish-gray, brightened by a splash of yellow on its rump that explains its other, irreverent name, "butterbutt." It's something of a dandy, going through seven or eight plumages in a lifetime, highlighted by a breeding-season outfit of blue-black with yellow throat, crown, rump and side patches.

The new arrivals most likely flew in from the Sierra Nevada, where they are the most common and widespread of warblers. But they coexist with a half-dozen other varieties of these gleaners, occupying different levels of pines and firs, nesting at different times and even feeding on different insects. The biologists call this adaptive specialization; just call it neighborliness.

The yellow-rumped warblers are now taking up residence in valley backyards, parks and river groves. They never seem to stop as they hustle about putting on fat for the winter, flitting through tree branches, circling out beyond the foliage, in quest of a gnat or fly, flashing their yellow tail lights for the alert observer.

Easterners tend to affect a superior air when it comes to warblers, since they may see 20 varieties in a day during the spring migration from the tropics. Never mind, we'll take the little yellow-rumps.

Yellow-rumped warbler is something of a dandy, donning seven or eight plumages in a lifetime.

Indian summer

FIVE SOOTY-BLACK COOTS paddled leisurely across a lagoon of the lower American River, their heads bobbing in a cha-cha-cha motion. In their wakes, they left widening V's on the glassy, green surface that bespoke a sunny, still day following the first autumn rain. It was Indian summer in the great valley.

Easterners might pooh-pooh the idea of California with its consistent weather having an Indian summer. But all the signs were there on this day, with the possible exception of a hazy atmosphere, which it's doubtful anyone will miss.

Coots—and the rest of nature— are oblivious to any debate over when Indian summer arrives.

There may be some difference of opinion on when Indian summer arrives. In the valley, it could be any time in October or November.

Early-day Indians used the sunny days to bring in the last of their crops, accounting for the origin of the name of this time of year. Along the American River, the Southern Maidus held an annual acorn dance after the first autumn rains to give thanks to the spirits of the mountains for the moisture to nourish the oaks that provided the staple of their diet.

Days of fasting took place before the dance to help prepare the way for thanking the spirits and for requesting a lush crop of acorns the next season. Indian summer, then, was a time when the Native Americans showed they did not take nature's bounty for granted.

Red caps

THIS IS THE BUSY SEASON for the gaudy, gregarious acorn woodpecker. Wherever oak trees grow in our valley and foothills, one is likely to see and hear it thumping its stout bill against tree trunks or branches.

All this busy work is aimed at assuring that it will eat well. It may be chiseling under the bark looking for burrowing grubs. Or it may be drilling holes in the tree into which it will shove acorns point-first, many more than it will ever need this winter.

If such food-storing habits are exaggerated, so is its appearance. Large white wing patches flash as it swoops from tree to tree. And the acorn woodpecker's head is a clown's mask—bright red topknot, white face, black head and yellow bib.

When the woodpecker is rapping on a tree, its stance is not unlike that of a telephone lineman. Each foot is equipped with four toes, two turning forward and two backwards, along with sharp tail feathers so it can hang on while leaning back. Its long tongue with a barbed tip can grab insects from under the bark, thereby contributing to the health of a live tree.

Unlike many other birds, the acorn woodpecker gathers in large families, and individuals greet each other with strange behavior. When two birds meet, they bow and scrape and let loose a harsh, squawking call. They nest in colonies and adults often enter the wrong tree cavity to feed another couple's young, all in a notable spirit of togetherness.

When the acorn woodpecker is rapping on a tree, it assumes the stance of a telephone lineman.

Low diver

A GREBE IS A STRANGE sort of bird. It looks and acts almost as if it was put together by a committee–a swanlike neck that is snowy white in front, black on top, stubby wings and tail, red eyes, and legs set so far back on its body it can't walk on land.

This is the western grebe, with its look-alike kin, the Clark's grebe, in a breath-holding family of diving birds. A friend tells of an encounter with one on Lake Natoma below Folsom Dam:

We were paddling our canoes near the shore when we spotted it floating out in the middle. Phil said, "I'll give a dollar to anyone who can make it fly." We started paddling toward it, and were about 50 yards away when it suddenly leaped forward and disappeared. After a minute it surfaced nearby and we paddled furiously toward it. Again it dived. This routine was repeated twice more before we gave up. The grebe may not be much for walking or flying, but it's some underwater swimmer.

Nature equips it well for its water habitat. A grebe's foot isn't webbed like a duck's, but rather has flat lobes on its toes that help propel it through the water. It has waterproof feathers, but it has the knack of "squeezing" air from the plumage so it can sink below the surface like a submarine.

Chances are that the Lake Natoma grebe spent the breeding season at a tule-lined lake in the Sierra Nevada. Anyone who has ever seen the courtship dance of a pair of western grebes isn't likely to forget it. They rise up as if on their toes and race side-by-side across the water, necks arched up and heads down, suggesting a Nureyev-Fonteyn pas de deux.

A western grebe's young are able to swim as soon as they hatch. But when they tire, they can cling to the back of their mother. They do this even when the mother has dived beneath the surface, trying to spear a small fish with her slender yellow-green bill. Nature is the great accommodator.

The grebe's legs are so far back on its body that it can't walk on land.

Hip, hip!

THE WILD ROSE is a waist-high, brambly shrub with unfriendly thorns and fragrant pink flowers that have gone to seed by now. But what a seed!

The seeds, or hips, range from orange to bright red, growing in clusters of four or five, and are a prized free food for anyone who finds them in the countryside. Of course, you will find them on garden roses, but the floral experts say that for best flower-production it's best not to let the hips form.

The wild rose is a shrub of many uses, as the native people learned. Carefully washed roots, petals and hips are used for a healthful tea. The skin and pulp of rose hips are used to make jams and jellies. There's even rose-hip soup.

Connoisseurs say rose hips have a light apple flavor but not everyone agrees. There is wide agreement, however, on their high content of scurvy-fighting Vitamin C. Three rose hips equal one orange in Vitamin C content, it's said.

Deer, squirrels, songbirds and rabbits also relish the leaves, flowers and buds of the wild rose, along with the safe cover of its prickly branches.

Perhaps Edward MacDowell had all these exemplary features in mind when he wrote *To a Wild Rose*, a musical ode to sip rose-hip tea by.

The wild rose is a shrub of many uses, as native Californians learned.

November

NOVEMBER IS a much-maligned month…unfairly, we believe.

Perhaps it all goes back to Thomas Hood's rhyme: *No shade, no shine, no butterflies, no bees; no fruits, no flowers, no leaves, no birds, November!* The 19th-century poet's dreary assessment may apply to the 11th month in his native England, but not in Northern California.

No shade? The evergreen interior live oak rises as high as 80 feet over the valley and foothills, its expansive foliage casting broad pools of shade.

No shine? The sun is a constant companion through much of the month, even as the aging year nears its end. No one gets rich selling overcoats around here this month.

No butterflies? Still making the scene are numerous species, such as the buckeye with its light brown wings and multi-colored eyespots.

No bees? A sunny November day brings them out, collecting nectar, producing honey and wax, getting ready for hibernation before turning to their spring task of pollinating fruit trees and other plants.

No fruits? The apples and cider available at roadside stands in the foothills should fill the bill.

No flowers? A few yellow blossoms of the star thistle are hanging on.

No leaves? The golden chain pendulums of the birches will do; even if they're not natives, they are used so widely in gardens and parks that they might as well be.

No birds? The ducks, geese and swans that are wintering on valley watercourses dispel any such myth.

Perhaps in Thomas Hood's England people must comfort themselves in November with memories of a warmer season. In our valley and foothills, November's bounty is the here and now.

Great flocks of migratory geese are a November spectacle in the valley.

Junco Weather

WE TALK ABOUT the various harbingers of spring such as the golden daffodil. But what of winter—how does nature signal its arrival in the the river region beyond the pale slanting rays of the sun?

For openers, we'll suggest the arrival of flocks of genial visitors from the mountains, dark-eyed juncos. If you've camped in the Sierra pine forests in summer, it's likely you were joined by these sparrow-sized birds with black head, neck and breast, brown back and wings, gray underparts and white outer-tail feathers.

In October and November, they head down to the foothills and valley, foraging for seeds and insects. Anyone with a backyard feeder knows these birds would rather pick up seeds spilled on the ground than perch on the feeder itself.

It's been said that the junco's black head and breast resemble the executioner's hood, but it ill-deserves such a comparison. We prefer the vision evoked by its other name, snowbird, earned by junco stay-behinds that scratch through the snow for seeds and burrow down for shelter at night.

In the valley now it is junco weather, a good time to offer a handout of bread crumbs and seeds to these handsome visitors to tide them over until May, when they will head back into the mountains to build their nests.

It's been said that the junco's black head and breast resemble the executioner's hood, but it ill-deserves such a comparison.

All-American Bird

WE KNOW MANY THINGS about the turkey, beginning with its star status on the Thanksgiving table, with savory stuffing, cranberries and pumpkin pie in supporting roles. We know that Ben Franklin favored the turkey for national bird, but it lost out to the bald eagle. And we know that modern turkey farmers learned to breed a smaller bird with a bigger chest than its rangy wild cousin.

But more difficult to discover is the origin of the wild turkey's name. It's a North American native, so the nation of Turkey can't claim credit for it. It might be assumed that the name sprang from the belief of early explorers that the America they found was Asia. But if that were so, wouldn't they have more logically named the bird a Cathay (China) hen?

Nor were matters clarified when the bird was given its scientific name *Meleagris*. The word literally means "guinea hen," a bird with no relation to the turkey. Long before the Spaniards arrived in North America, natives of what was to be the Southwest and Mexico had domesticated the turkey for its metallic green, copper and bronze feathers, not for its flesh.

The Spaniards took turkeys back to Europe, and early English settlers brought them to the East Coast of North America where, it turned out, the woods were full of native turkeys.

Along with deer and buffalo, the turkey played a key role by sustaining westward-moving Americans as they tamed the wilderness. Today Sacramentans may catch a glimpse of a flock of wild turkeys slipping through the underbrush of the Sierra foothills and the American River Parkway, especially around the Effie Yeaw Nature Center in Ancil Hoffman Park.

With so many redeeming features, it is difficult to understand why "turkey" has become an epithet for an unpleasant person. It may not be the prettiest creature alive, but it will always be an all-American bird to many, especially on the festive board at Thanksgiving.

Natives of the southwest and Mexico domesticated the gaudy turkey for its feathers, not its flesh.

Special days

THERE ARE TWO DAYS to savor when winter's first real rainstorm arrives over the Sacramento Valley. The first is the day when the rain makes its debut and washes away the dust that has gathered in the air during the dry summer and fall of our Mediterranean climate. The "silver hosannas of rain" caress a pine tree, sending drops sliding down the needles of one branch onto the needles below until finally they land on the dried golden needles covering the ground. A heavy pine fragrance is released, carrying one in spirit back to the mountains.

After winter's baptism comes the very special day when the storm moves on and the sun reappears. From the city, the whitened Sierra Nevada appears diamond-clear against the eastern horizon. And in the foreground the sun sparkles off the slow-moving river, a tinselly panoply of lights.

A raft of gulls loafs through the Thanksgiving holiday on a sand bar, while a few coots paddle industriously around them. Warblers down from the mountains dart out from their perches in a leafless tree to snare some of the gnats that have suddenly appeared in great numbers after the storm.

Willow leaves have turned yellow, but are hanging tough before giving up the ghost for the winter. Most of the lanky telegraph plants are dried brown and tilted at crazy angles, but in sheltered areas a few survive, with daisy-like flowers lending a note of color to the wintry scene.

The pesky star thistle spreads in all directions, tempting one to call down the wrath of the gods on whoever was responsible for introducing it to the valley from Europe in the 19th century.

Then rising from the thistle's drab presence comes the sweet song of the meadowlark. The bubbling melody rises and falls, and for a moment this day-after-the-storm seems like the first day of spring.

After winter's baptism comes the very special day when the storm moves on and the sun reappears.

Tundra swans head for the delta to escape Arctic winters.

The orphan

THE STATELY SWAN paddled leisurely against the current of the lower American River. This, the largest waterfowl, overshadowed nearby mallards and mergansers. It didn't really belong here, making the sight all the more interesting.

The ash-gray neck, longer than the snowy body, marked this tundra swan as an immature bird, one that was born this year. Normally it would have been with a large flock of swans spending the winter gleaning leftover grain near delta shallows at least an hour's flight away. We can only speculate on why it was on this river in the middle of suburbia.

It entered the world last summer, perhaps on Alaska's barren Arctic coast, hatched from one of a half-dozen eggs in a nest made of water plants and swan's down. By October, as temperatures began dropping, the young bird, or *cygnet*, was ready to join its parents, siblings and other swans on the long flight down the Pacific flyway.

Pushed along by increasingly cold weather, the swan family would have flown south in V's or diagonal lines, necks outstretched, broad wings propelling them through the skies at 40 mph or more. As leaders of the flock took turns at the wind-buffeting point of the procession, the air filled with honking sounds, ranging from deep bass notes to shrill tones like clarinets.

Whatever it is that steers swans in the right direction— geographical features, the stars or magnetic influence—a great many find their way to a favorite feeding spot on Victoria Island in the Sacramento-San Joaquin River Delta, where 10,000 or more may gather in winter.

But somewhere along the way, disaster may have struck the family of the lone American River swan. Its parents, who mated for life, may have fallen victim to fowl cholera or a fog-shrouded transmission line. The young swan lost its way, and now it is alone.

But it likely will search out another flock in the delta or in the San Joaquin Valley, calling out with muffled, musical whistles. Swans are intolerant of intruders during breeding season on the far north tundra, but down here they surely will adopt this orphan and let it stay with them until it's time for the return to the Arctic in March. They will take care of one of their own, once he finds them.

December

DECEMBER, Whittier wrote, was a brief day when the sun "rose cheerless over hills of gray." Here in the Sacramento Vallley, December can be an incomparable day, a golden-blonde, blue-eyed day that makes us feel superior to the poor fellow stamping his feet in the snow while waiting for the tow-truck to come and get his car started.

December is the offical start of winter. It's the month with the shortest day and the longest night, when the sun reaches the solstice and appears to have gone farthest south. It's the frosty month, the adding-up-accounts month.

December is admiring the nuthatch, titmouse and junco suddenly visible on the bare-boned elm. It is also the month to rake up leaves or, as we would prefer, just watch the wind send them tumbling across the ground like a cavalry charge.

December is turning over a log and discovering a lizard, brown with black spots, and wriggling, annoyed at having its winter siesta disturbed. A man who knows says it's a Gilbert's skink, which has a novel defense when attacked: Its tail breaks off readily and continues to wriggle, diverting the predator's attention as the lizard escapes. Sometimes.

December is two red-tailed hawks buzzing a golden eagle perched on a fence post until, good and ready, it spreads its wings and ponderously takes flight.

December is a rusty-breasted say's phoebe snaring mosquitoes and gnats along a fence-row, occupying the same food niche as a western kingbird. The kingbird has gone south for the winter and the phoebe is visiting from the north.

December is the deep-red berries of the toyon shrub, holiday festivities and visions of sugar plums. And a prayer for peace on earth, good will to all.

The stately golden eagle seems ponderous in flight.

Gray day

EVERYTHING SEEMS to slow down with the arrival of the tule fog in the big valley. Cars don't move so fast and air traffic sometimes doesn't move at all.

The fog may be unfairly maligned. Certainly it can chill the bones and imperil the unwary, but it offers a welcome contrast in a region conspicuous for its lack of seasonal extremes.

Out along the river, nature's metronome lapses into slow motion under a cottony blanket of moisture. There's no wind and the tall cottonwoods cast shadows that shimmer on the water, outlined by the pale light of the luminous disc that is the sun.

Several head-bobbing coots trail a widening V in the placid water, proclaiming their domains with one-note squawks. And the deeply-lobed leaves of a valley oak flutter to the ground, a leisurely disrobing by the valley's most majestic native plant.

It's a little more than mist now, this condensation of warm air radiating from the earth and meeting the chilly air draining into the valley from the mountains and foothills. The moisture in the warm air turns into droplets of water as it meets the cooler air, creating a miniature cloud.

Still, fog is a monochrome of grayness and a canopy of quietness; it is a cool hand caressing the skin.

Out along the river, nature's metronome lapses into slow motion under a cottony blanket of moisture.

Watch the birdies

IN THE 19TH CENTURY it was a Christmas tradition to rise early and head for field and forest for a "bird shoot." Then in 1899 a handful of birdwatchers launched a variation of the ritual by heading out to hunt the birds with binoculars, pencil and paper.

Now, on a certain day between December 20 and January 2, tens of thousands of Audubon Society members and others spread out in teams in more than 1,250 areas from Alaska to Central America in a dawn-to-dusk tabulation of the total number and species of birds.

Most of them consider the Christmas bird count the high point of their birding year, a test of their enthusiasm carried out rain or shine. The census has some scientific value because groups return to the same areas each year and their statistics provide conclusions about bird population growth, migratory patterns and the like.

Many birders consider rigorous Christmas counts—of waterfowl in this case—a true test of their enthusiasm.

Competition is friendly but intense as each team vies to see which one tallies the most species. In one recent year, Sacramento Audubon members topped the nation for seeing the most kestrels, barn owls, red-tailed hawks, burrowing owls (a tie), yellow-billed magpies, northern flickers, water pipits, western meadowlarks, American goldfinches and savannah sparrows.

To some, the Christmas bird count may seem a masochistic way to spend the holidays and, indeed, for many birders their first Christmas count is their last. But whether it's a source of pride or despair, most will agree that it's a day to remember.

The cycle

THE MIRACLE HAD ITS ORIGIN four years ago in a nest of loose stones just above a riffle in the American River near Rancho Cordova. No parent was around as the pink, pea-sized egg lay next to several thousand others, but oxygen carried by the fast-moving water offered the necessary incubation. After 55 or so days, the egg hatched.

The young fish looked like a tadpole, with the pinkish yolk sac that provided its nourishment. It wriggled up through the gravel and for the next month lived off its yolk sac until the sac was finally absorbed. By then the organism had taken on the appearance it would carry through most of its life—a sleek, silver-sided fish aptly called the chinook or king salmon.

The fingerling fed on tiny forms of life in the stream until some instinct told it there was more bountiful sustenance hundreds of miles away. And so she began her long journey, traveling mostly at night to keep out of the way of gulls and larger fish.

The salmon reached the Pacific and headed north. She fattened on vast amounts of "pink feed," a sort of tiny shrimp, and squid and smaller fish.

And she managed to avoid her enemies such as the sea lion, the shark, the eel-like lamprey, and the spoons and hooks of trolling fishermen.

By this fall, our salmon had grown to 22 pounds. She had achieved maturity and it was time to keep another date with her destiny, the regeneration of her species. By now she was living off the Oregon coast, but she headed back south, past the mouths of the Klamath, the Smith and Eel rivers, ignoring Redwood Creek, the Mad and Mattole rivers.

Finally she was drawn through the Golden Gate and into San Francisco Bay, on through Carquinez Strait to the delta and the

The miracle of the salmon begins and ends in the gravel beds of the American River.

*Salmon: renewing
the cycle with a
fabled fighting spirit.*

Sacramento River. Was it her acute sense of smell that brought her to her ancestral home on the American? Perhaps.

By now her silver sides had turned an ominous blackish, and although she did not feed, she thrashed the water with the fabled fighting spirit of her species. She reached the spawning area close to her place of birth and began clearing a nest with a pumping motion of her body that roiled the surface. She deposited some eggs, which were immediately fertilized by a waiting male that also was nearing the end of its life span. The process was repeated several times, and each time the dislodged rocks of a new nest provided a protective cover for the previous deposit of eggs. For the next few days the spawned-out fish drifted listlessly downstream.

Life went on along the river, as a flotilla of goldeneyes paddled near her, flame-red wild grape leaves laced the far cliff and the rattling cry of a kingfisher echoed upstream. There in the shallows off Rancho Cordova, the chinook salmon died, victorious in accomplishing what nature had driven her to do.

Photography credits

Cover: Mergansers, © George Turner
Inside covers: River, © George Turner

1:   Discovery Park, © Tom Myers
3:   Dandelion, © George Turner
5:   Indian pink, © George Turner
7:   Clouds, © George Turner
9:   Lizard, © George Turner
11: Beaver, © Jim Louthian
13: Trees in winter, © Tom Myers
14: Coots, © George Turner
17: Sandhill cranes, © George Turner
18: Elderberries, © George Turner
21: White-tailed kite, © George Turner
22: Steelhead, © Tom Myers
25: River scene, © Tom Myers
26: Mergansers, © George Turner
29: Wood duck, © George Turner
30: Mule deer, © George Turner
32: Titmouse, © George Turner
35: Mourning cloak, © Tom Myers
36: Incense cedar, © Ron Pickup
38: Hummingbird, © George Turner
41: Vetch, © George Turner
43: Bee, © George Turner
44: Horehound, © Peter Hayes
47: Baby mockingbird, © Tom Myers
48: Northern flicker, © George Turner
51: Clouds, © George Turner

52: Ladybug, © Tom Myers
55: Oats, © George Turner
56: Lupine, © Tom Myers
59: Clover, © Tom Myers
60: Vernal pool, © Tom Myers
63: Poppies, © Tom Myers
65: Great horned owl, © Tom Myers
66: Hawk, © George Turner
69: Mallard hen, © George Turner
70: Cottonwoods, © Tom Myers
73: Oaks, © Tom Myers
75: Sunflowers, © George Turner
77: Pipevine swallowtail, © George Turner
     Dutchman's pipe, © Jo Smith
79: Wildflowers, © Jo Smith
81: Dragonfly, © Tom Myers
82: Bullfrog, © Tom Myers
85: Quail, © Jack Wilburn
86: Pond turtle, © Jack Wilburn
89: Canoe, © Tom Myers
91: Blackberries, © George Turner
92: N.F. American, © Mark Leder-Adams/
     Rapidshooters
95: Field, © Tom Myers
96: Lorquin's admiral, © Jack Wilburn
99: Killdeer, © George Turner
101: Poison oak, © George Turner
102: Orb weaver, © Tom Myers
105: Green heron, © George Turner

106: Woods, © Tom Myers
109: Cattails, © Jeff Myers
111: Butterfly, © Tom Myers
112: Yellow-rumped warbler, © Jack Wilburn
114: Coot, © Tom Myers
117: Acorn woodpecker, © Jack Wilburn
118: Grebes, © George Turner
121: Rose hips, © Tom Myers
123: Geese, © George Turner
124: Junco, © Jack Wilburn
127: Wild turkey, © George Turner
129: Gulls, © George Turner
130: Swans, © George Turner
132: Golden eagle, © George Turner
135: Fog in trees, © Tom Myers
136: Ducks, © George Turner
139: Salmon, © Tom Myers
140: Salmon, © Tom Myers
143: Discovery Park, © Tom Myers

Photograph of Peter J. Hayes © by Jo Smith
Photograph of Tom Myers © by Sally Myers
Photograph of George Turner © by Cora Turner

Back cover: Details from pages 14, 63, 82, 89

The contributors

Peter J. Hayes reported and edited for
United Press (later United Press
International) in San Francisco, Spokane,
Seattle and Anchorge before joining
The Sacramento Union as an editor in 1966.
During his 25-year career with *The Union,*
he shared with readers his appreciation of
the American River habitat in more than
200 editorials. He was honored by the
Sacramento Audubon Society and the
Save the American River Association for his
support of the American River Parkway.

Tom Myers and his wife, Sally Myers, share a career in free-lance photography
that includes photo credits in *National Geographic* and *Newsweek*. Their
pictures have appeared in books, advertisements and travel publications, and
on album covers, posters and greeting cards. Their collection of 500,000 color
transparencies includes pictures of the Pacific Coast from San Diego to Alaska.

Tom Myers's photographs
have appeared in 50
international exhibitions, and
he has won top awards from
the California Press
Photographer's Association.
He can be contacted at
(916) 443-8886.

George Turner, a former commercial pilot, became hooked on nature
photography during the 1970s after spotting egret rookeries while flying near
Colusa Wildlife Refuge. His photographs have appeared in the *New York
Times* and national magazines. He is a corporate photographer and
videographer for a Sacramento public utility and a certificated Website
designer. Mr. Turner designed
the sites of the American
River Natural History
Association, www.arnha.org,
and Effie Yeaw Nature Center,
www.effieyeaw.org.
He can be reached at
gturner@wildlegacy.com.

ALSO CONTRIBUTING:

Jack Wilburn, formerly an Aerojet rocket scientist and Sacramento Bee
weekly nature columnist, is a free-lance nature photographer, writer and tour
guide who also develops specialized photo equipment. His photo credits have
appeared in *National Geographic* and other respected magazines as well as
textbooks, encyclopedias and field guides.

A special thanks to photographers **Mark Leder-Adams, Jim Louthian,
Jeff Myers, Ron Pickup** and **Jo Smith** for the use of their work.

Index